COLLINS AURA GARDEN HANDBOOKS

ALPINES

KENNETH A. BECKETT

D0325217

COLLINS

Products mentioned in this book

Benlate* + 'Activex'	contains	benomyl
'Picket'	contains	permethrin
'Sybol'	contains	pirimiphos-methyl

Products marked thus '*Sybol*' are trade marks of Imperial Chemical Industries plc
*Benlate** is a registered trade mark of Du Pont's
Read the label before you buy: use pesticides safely.

Editor Emma Johnson
Designers James Marks, Steve Wilson
Picture research Moira McIlroy

This edition first published 1988 by
William Collins Sons & Co Ltd
London · Glasgow · Sydney
Auckland · Toronto · Johannesburg

British Library Cataloguing in Publication Data

Beckett, Kenneth A.
    Alpines.——(Collins Aura garden handbooks).
    1. Rock plants 2. Alpine garden plants
    I. Title
    635.9′672   SB421

ISBN 0–00–412372–7

Photoset by Bookworm Typesetting
Printed and bound in Hong Kong by Dai Nippon Printing
Company

Front cover: Gentiana sino-ornata
Back cover: Sempervivum tectorum
Both by the Harry Smith Horticultural Photographic Collection

CONTENTS

INTRODUCTION

Miniature versions of all kinds of things, animal, vegetable and mineral, have long had a wide appeal. Tiny plants in particular are popular, as the steadily growing membership of societies devoted to alpines and bonsai testifies. They offer the gardener a wide variety of plant form as well as blossoms of every shape, colour and hue, often in astonishing prodigality. Being small, a large number of these plants can be fitted with ease into the tiniest garden, and no other group of plants offers such variety for the balcony or window box. Naturally small plants occur in all climates and habitats, but the hardier sorts are native to mountains and dry, rocky or sandy places, often near the sea. Collectively they are known as alpines or rock plants, though technically many are neither.

Alpines True alpine plants are natives of mountain heights above the tree zone. Except in very arid climates, the slopes of mountains are naturally covered with trees up to an altitude where extreme exposure and cold prevent their growth. Beyond this point there is usually a zone of dwarf trees or shrubs which fades out into steep rock slopes and bare outcrops open to strong winds and extremes of heat and cold. In the arctic this region starts at sea level, but moving southwards it is pushed higher and higher up the mountains. In the tropical mountains of Africa the alpine flora starts at above 3000m (10,000ft).

Alpines have evolved to withstand extremes of climate, often with sudden fluctuations – intense heat during the day as the sun beats down through the thin mountain air and often freezing temperatures at night, even during the growing and flowering season. In winter the plants are exposed to temperatures well below freezing point and they may be buried for months on end under a blanket of snow.

To withstand all these conditions, alpines have developed congested growth forms, usually variations on a theme of mat, hummock and cushion, composed of small, often hard-textured leaves. In some cases, as for example in *Androsace sarmentosa*, the winter leaves are tiny and arranged in tight rosettes, while the summer leaves are many times larger and more loosely arranged. Other plants die down at the onset of winter. Quite often the whole plant is covered with woolly hair, which is a further protection against the elements. The higher up you go into the mountains or towards the poles, the shorter the summer and thus the growing season for plant life. Alpines overcome this limitation in

two ways, by being able to grow at low temperatures and by growing very fast as soon as warmer weather arrives.

When plants that have adapted to this rigorous way of life are brought down to the average lowland garden there can be problems of cultivation. In Europe and parts of North America, the winters can be mild and wet just at the time when the alpines should be experiencing a dry, cold resting period, often under thick snow. In general, the higher an alpine plant lives the less easy it is to cultivate in the lowlands. Happily, there are many mountain plants from the edge of the alpine region and below which are perfectly easy to grow; some of the best so-called alpine plants are of this origin. True high alpine plants test the skill of the cultivator and are not for the beginner. On the other hand, once experience of growing the easier plants is gained, the gardener may welcome the additional satisfaction of growing the rarer varieties from the high peaks.

FAR LEFT *Morisia monanthos*, native to Corsica and Sardinia where it inhabits sandy ground from sea level to 1200m.
LEFT The twinflower (*Linnaea borealis americana*) is a charming mat-forming woodlander ideal for the shady nooks on a rock garden.
BELOW Natural rock outcrops in the Swiss Alps, the home of many small plants, including the alpine rose.

Rock plants This covers all the little plants native to the lowlands and open areas on hills and lower mountain slopes. A surprising number of these come from cliffs and rocky slopes, usually where the soil is too poor or the rainfall too low to support a cover of trees or scrub. Among familiar examples grown as basic rock plants are various kinds of stonecrops (*sedum*), thymes (*thymus*), stone cresses (*aethionema*), madworts (*alyssum*), stork-bills (*erodium*) and gromwells (*lithospermum*). Seaside habitats give us the highly useful thrift (*armeria*) and its colour forms, the double sea campion (*Silene maritima* 'Flora Pleno'), the ever-popular *Morisia monanthos* (*M. hypogaea*) and several others.

Curiously enough, woodland areas are the home of quite a number of small plants much suited to the shady parts of rock gardens and beds. Well known genera are *hepatica, primula, meconopsis, linnaea* and *shortia*. Even the comparative lushness of stream and lakeside yields a handful of plants few rock gardens would want to be without. The monkey-flower or musk genus *mimulus*, is perhaps the best example along with the allied *mazus*, and several of the primulas.

As can be seen from this brief survey, rock and alpine plants offer a splendid diversity, both in form, colour and cultural requirements. There is no garden where at least some of them will not thrive and look attractive.

Using alpine and rock plants

Until comparatively recently, the accepted way of growing rock and alpine plants was to plant them on a properly constructed rock garden which itself had some aesthetic appeal. The primary consideration was to produce a fragment of mountain scenery in the garden, suitably embellished with a selection of authentic plants. Gradually as the interest and beauty of the plants became the main reason for doing this, it was realized that a rock garden was not necessarily the best place for alpine plants.

An ancillary factor in the waning interest in rock garden construction is the expense of importing suitable stone from far-away quarries to lowland garden sites. Furthermore, the construction of a convincing rock garden requires skill, a certain flair, and the ability to move heavy blocks of stone without injuring yourself.

Moraines and screes are very much a part of mountain scenery and early on in the history of the rock garden these features were reproduced in miniature. The idea was to provide a suitable home for certain plants which, in the wild, are primarily found growing in such habitats. Moraines proved difficult

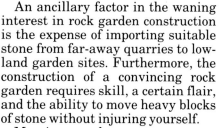

to construct and maintain efficiently, but screes were easier to construct and provided perfect growing conditions for many alpine plants. A scree bed can be any size and shape and need not have an adjacent rock garden. Sited by the edge of a lawn or patio for example, it can make an attractive and satisfying feature. A natural development of the scree is the raised bed and this can make a splendid feature or focal point. The vertical sides of a raised bed are equivalent to retaining or dry walls, which provide ideal planting sites for cliff dwellers or plants that need to be kept dry around their collars – for example lewisia. Dry walls

around a terrace should be similarly used to advantage. A free-standing dry wall makes an unusual 'hedge' or divider (for example, to separate the food kitchen garden from the rest of the garden). In effect, it is a linear raised bed with two vertical faces. Effectively planted, it makes an unusual and attractive feature.

In the wild, the small plants often form a close mosaic and this effect can easily be reproduced in the garden if the soil is well drained or can be made so. In effect, the rock and alpine plants are used like mini-herbaceous perennials. Although the idea is not a new one – it is much like the alpine lawn – it has taken that well-known pioneer in innovation, Alan Bloom of Bressingham, to popularize this way of using alpines. Ground level beds of this sort can be made in a lawn or in place of a very small lawn. Alternatively, they can form a broad edging around a large bed of larger perennials or shrubs. Setting out rock plants to alleviate the monotony of a large paved area has long been an accepted gardening practice. It is also well worth considering as a feature in its own right, to replace a very small lawn or to form a broad edging to a drive, patio or larger lawn.

Sinks and troughs are natural homes for tiny plants and their popularity for this purpose is phenomenal. Constructed and planted as a miniature rock garden, a sink makes a most appealing feature for a patio, terrace or courtyard, or anywhere else in the garden where a small focal point is needed.

FAR LEFT TOP
Mazus reptans.
FAR LEFT BOTTOM
The fairy foxglove
Erinus alpinus, a true
mountain plant.

LEFT Part of an
expertly constructed
rock garden with a
scree bed.

THE ROCK GARDEN

The definition of a rock garden is a composition of rocks and soil constructed as a home for the many small plants that naturally inhabit stony, open places. It will probably never be known who built the first recognisable rock garden in Britain, but one of the earliest and most remarkable was made about 1830 for Lady Broughton at Hoole House near Chester. It was, as far as one can judge from written evidence, a scale model of the Valley of Chamonix and it was planted with a selection of rare and beautiful alpines.

The most famous of the first modern rock gardens, built primarily to display alpine plants, was made by the nursery firm of James Backhouse and Son of York in 1859. This firm also listed many alpine plants in its catalogue.

Rocks have for centuries been a primary feature in the gardens of China and Japan. Indeed, in these countries the rocks were more important than the plants, having both symbolical significance and aesthetic appeal. There is little doubt that oriental gardens, particularly those of Japan, provided inspiration for the British and European attempts at modern rock gardens.

Although nowadays the emphasis is on a suitable home for rock and alpine plants, the rock garden itself should be an attractive setting for them. If at all possible, natural stone should be used and placed in such a way as to simulate natural rock outcrops. To achieve this, sloping ground is required either in the form of a natural hillside or an artificial mound. This requirement is the basis for the two main kinds of rock garden constructed today – raised and sunken. The raised garden is the most naturalistic, outcrops being constructed in a slope as they would appear in nature. For sunken or flat gardens you can achieve height by

RIGHT Horizontal outcrops in a sunken rock garden, with the dwarf bloom *Cytisus × beanii*.
ABOVE A traditional stone garden in Japan, where rocks are more important than plants.

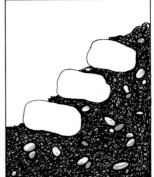

1. Mark out the shape of the rock garden, using thick rope or a length of hose; then remove turf. Dig around the outside of the bed, throwing the soil into the centre to make a mound.

2. After firming the mound and contouring it to shape, excavate the base to take the first layer or strata of rocks.

3. Place the rocks and make sure they are firmly in position. Pull soil down from above to half cover the lower layer, then lay the next layer, and so on.

excavating soil and throwing it up into a mound or series of mounds with sunken paths between. Making a pond can form the beginnings of a rock garden of this sort. The only way to build a convincing rock garden without excavating is to buy soil to create the necessary mounds (see also Outcrop Garden below). Although on a massive scale, the Rock Garden at the Royal Horticultural Society Gardens, Wisley, is a fine example of a raised garden, while those at Kew Gardens and the University Botanic Gardens, Cambridge show what can be achieved on a flat site.

Unless you are lucky enough to live near a quarry, natural stone can be an expensive item. It should therefore be chosen with care. If possible it is best to use the rock indigenous to the area you live in. Not only will it be cheaper, but it will be more compatible with the landscape. In flat clay areas it is best to use one of the sandstones or sandy limestones with flat cleavage lines; towering masses of water-worn limestone look very out of place in

such sites. This is, of course, a 'council of perfection' and if your first consideration is growing alpines well, any suitable stone can be used. Even lumps of concrete can be used if that is the only 'stone' obtainable. It is surprising what can be done with an unpromising material if it is used skillfully.

Siting and soil The ideal site for a rock garden should be open to the sky and, if possible, sheltered from drying north and east winds which can damage premature young growth arising after a mild, snowless winter. A site near trees is not recommended, especially if they are the deciduous sort with large leaves that can cover tiny plants with a soggy layer in autumn and winter.

Most plants from mountainous and other rocky areas require a well-drained soil if they are to thrive. Although mountain tops and flanks can experience high rainfall, the rocky nature of the soil ensures that there is no moisture stagnating around the roots. Lowland stony areas can be relatively dry and the

11

soils there are free-draining. This must be borne in mind when you are constructing a rock garden on a flat site.

If the soil is clay it may be necessary to lay one or more tile drains across the site, leading them to a ditch, pond or bog if these are available features in the garden or can be made at the same time. Alternatively, you may have to dig a sump to take the drainage water.

Any turf must be removed and stacked nearby. After this the top soil should be dug out at least the depth of one spade. At this stage the main rock areas or outcrops must be marked out and the sub-soil be-

tween, or to one side of them, dug out and put in mounds up to form the cores of the outcrops. The sub-soil mounds must be firmed as they are made, then covered with a thick layer of top-soil, also firmed. If the top-soil is sticky or of a very fine silty nature it is worthwhile mixing it with gritty sand and peat before using it to bed around the stone and fill planting pockets. The stone can now be moved into position. First lay out the largest pieces to form the outline and foundations of an outcrop. Each stone must be bedded firmly with up to half its bulk beneath the soil and tilting slightly in towards the centre to provide

ABOVE Part of a sandstone rock garden. **RIGHT** Skillful use of water in limestone rock garden.

stability and to direct rainwater down to the roots. Some of the mound should be pulled down to cover the inner faces of the rocks, and the next layer bedded in and so on. The upper layer rocks must be buried by half to two-thirds of their bulk and firmed by ramming. Each layer should be set back from the one beneath to aid stability and to make planting fairly easy.

It is permissible, and even desirable in the larger rock garden, to create one or more vertical bluffs to add character to the rock work. There are some alpines that grow well in vertical rock faces or look particularly effective there, for example *Saxifraga callosa (lingulata)* and *S. longifolia*. The limit is usually three layers high, but here and there a fourth layer may be used effectively, depending on the overall size of the rock garden. As far as possible the stone should be laid to create a natural effect. Where the rocks have clearly marked strata bands, these should be kept in one plane, either horizontal or slightly tilted as in nature. During construction, plenty of ledges and soil pockets must be provided for the plants. If vertical faces are planned it is worth organising young plants and

LEFT Some of the garden features ideal as homes for rock and alpine plants. Around a paved area are a dry wall, a small rock garden and a sink.

inserting these in crevices as building proceeds. Planting in such positions is difficult after construction.

Raised rock garden Building on a sloping site follows a similar pattern of soil preparation as outlined above, though there should be no drainage problems. Any turf and top-soil is removed where the rock outcrops are to go. If there are several outcrops, the first should be at the bottom of the slope, with the rest working upwards. Ideally, the lowest outcrops should be the largest and composed of the biggest rocks.

Planting Whatever the natural soil is like it is advisable to prepare the larger pockets for special plants. For example, if the rock is a non-limy sandstone and lime-hating plants such as cassiope and phyllodoce are favoured, the planting pockets should be largely of peat. If, like many saxifrages, the plants are lime lovers, then the soil must be well laced with limestone grit.

Apart from the vertical crevices, and perhaps other narrow planting ledges, setting out the young plants should not take place until the rock work is complete. The younger the plants, the better. Indeed, there is much to be said for setting out well-grown seedling and rooted cuttings. It is best to avoid severely root-bound specimens which often dry out before new roots can grow out into the surrounding soil and are then difficult to water properly. After planting, a mulch of stone chippings helps to conserve moisture and discourage weed seedlings. Afterwards, weeding must be regularly attended for it is all too easy for small, choice alpines to be smothered by fast-growing weeds such as chickweed and annual meadow grass.

SCREES AND MORAINES

By the weathering action of heat, cold and rain, mountain rocks slowly but surely crumble. Gravity carries the fragments down the slopes, at the bottom of which the larger lumps settle. The smaller stuff builds up behind and after many millennia the familiar, narrow fan-shaped screes are formed.

Screes then are made of rock fragments of all sizes, from massive boulders to fine dust. From time to time they shift and slip and are generally unstable. They would appear to be the most unpromising of all habitats and yet a variety of alpine plants not only grow there, but are seldom found elsewhere. For example, that superb mountain nasturtium, *Tropaeolum polyphyllum*, grows only in the vast Andean screes of Chile and Argentina.

Glaciers grind away the rocks as they move down their high mountain valleys. They also collect scree material from the slopes above. This glacial detritus is known as moraine. It is basically the same as scree, but more evenly mixed. In the summer, melted snow and ice flows beneath the great banks of detritus that terminates a moraine. As with scree, this curious habitat also has its quota of plants, some of them in common with the scree.

Early in the history of rock gardening attempts were made to make miniature replicas of screes and moraines in order to grow the plants native to them. Formulating a scree or moraine mixture and making a sloping bed against larger rocks was not difficult, but organising a flow of water beneath presented problems and proved expensive of time and labour. Happily it was soon found that moraine plants (if they would grow anywhere in cultivation) would grow just as happily in a scree bed and the

moraine garden passed into history.

Screes have some lowland relatives in the form of gravel terraces by rivers and streams, and the vast shingle beaches by the sea. Both of these habitats grow some attractive garden plants – thrift, sea poppy and seakale are three British examples. Shingle and scree provide much the same sort of habitat for alpine, mountain and lowland plants that need the sharpest drainage to stay neat, floriferous and healthy. Imitations of both are easy to make in the garden.

Scree materials In the past many formulae were tried, each originator claiming that theirs was the best. The real answer is that many mixtures can be successful and this allows us to use whatever basic material is easiest and cheapest to acquire. The main ingredient of a scree can be clean road grit or gravel, ideally not less than 12mm (½in) grade. Screened clinkers from coal or coke furnaces is another possibility,but they need stacking out in the open for at least six months to weather. A thorough soaking with water from a hose shortens the process. Sometimes the fragments and dust in stone quarries are available and these can be used if not too coarse (at least 50 per cent should be of 12mm (½in) gravel size or less).

Commercial limestone chippings make a good basis for a scree devoted to lime-loving plants. To these basic ingredients must be added some soil and peat. A successful all-purpose mix is three parts of bulk basic gravel or stone, one part loam or garden soil and one part peat. In the wetter areas, for example where the rainfall is in excess of 75cm (30in) per annum, an extra one or two parts of basic material is worthwhile. As soon as the ingredients are roughly mixed together it is ready to be laid.

A good site for a scree is at the edge or on a slope of a rock garden. It can however be in a bed by itself. If the soil beneath is clay or a heavy, water-retentive loam, the scree should sit on the surface supported by rocks or baulks of timber. It must be at least 30cm (1ft) thick. A sloping site of not more than 30 degrees, is ideal. On well-drained soils the scree bed can be partially or wholly sunken. If a rock garden and scree are planned together, the excavated soil will make a rock mound. On well-drained soil the thickness of the scree mixture can be reduced to 20-25cm (8-10in) and a flat site is best though it can be slightly sloping. When in position the scree mixture should be lightly trodden, raked level then topped off with about 4cm (1½in) of the basic material only. If the scree covers more than 3sq.m (3sq.yd) a few pieces of natural stone, pushed into the surface, will improve its appearance.

Shingle bed Most of the comments on scree beds apply here. On the whole shingle beds are simpler to construct and are best for plants needing a very sharply drained rooting medium, low in nutrients, to maintain compact growth. The basic material is washed beach shingle or the similar material from gravel pits, such as water-worn or partially worn pebbles about 12-25mm (½-1in) grade, though smaller can be used. A cheap way of obtaining this is to buy what ballast dealers call drive gravel. This is roughly mixed at five parts bulk to one part soil, or a mixture of peat and soil. Unless the site is a very poorly drained clay, the shingle bed is best sunken. Raised or sunken it must be at least 30cm (1ft) deep. If drainage is slow, start with a 15cm (6in) layer of hardcore.

When planting, some extra soil or compost should be worked into the shingle around the root balls to aid establishment of the new root system. With extra soil added, a shingle bed can be used for scree plants. Indeed, in the garden the two have much the same function – both benefit from an annual dressing of bonemeal at 90g (3oz) per sq.m (yd) in late winter.

A colourful scree garden built on a natural rocky slope in the Lake District. | Imitation scree can be made in the garden.

15

RAISED BEDS

Raising a bed above the ground serves three primary purposes – providing an area of free-draining soil where there may have been little or none before, reducing the need to bend low when weeding and planting, and bringing the smaller plants nearer to eye-level so that they can be appreciated more.

All these purposes are very relevant to the growing of rock and alpine plants. Not surprisingly, we owe the development of the raised bed to enthusiasts for these plants. It has now reached the point where raised beds are accepted as a substitute for the traditional style rock garden. Indeed many growers prefer a raised bed to a rock garden as the tighter control on soil and situation enables them to have more success with the so-called 'difficult' plants.

Siting The same considerations apply to raised beds as to siting a rock garden or scree. However, whereas there are few perfect sites for the rock garden and scree, a raised bed can be made almost anywhere there is sufficient light. For example it looks well against a wall, the protection of which enables the cultivation of the less hardy rock plants. It can be placed near trees if you are concentrating on the shade-loving alpines and small ferns.

Construction About 30cm (1ft) is the lowest effective elevation for a raised bed, but 60-90cm (2-3ft) provides the best for the three purposes described above. More than 90cm (3ft) in height can create stability problems during construction. Three types of building material can be used – brick, stone and timber. If a formal square or oblong bed is required then brick should be considered, but it needs cementing if it is more than 30cm (1ft) high. Natural

stone, such as chunky pieces of sandstone or limestone, allows for the greatest flexibility of design and has the greatest aesthetic appeal in association with the plants. Dressed stone blocks are used in the same way as bricks and they look better, but they are very expensive.

Timber can be used formally or informally. Baulks of timber (for example, old railway sleepers), though far from elegant can be used to make a formal bed easily and

ABOVE A cross section through a raised bed: note drainage at base, though only needed on poorly drained sites. Above this is the growing mixture (see page 17), with a topping of fine gravel. RIGHT An effectively planted raised bed with yellow flax, alyssum, erysimum, dianthus etc.

efficiently. Curving cut sections of tree trunks make decorative informal beds, but the bark eventually decays and sloughs off and the chinks in between harbour woodlice, slugs and snails.

Before starting to build, the site must be freed from any persistent perennial weeds, if necessary with the aid of weedkiller containing glyphosate. The area must then be levelled and the outline of the bed marked out. If the bed is a formal shape this is easily done with small stakes and string. Informal beds can be shaped out with a length of hosepipe or rope. Oval or bean-shaped beds are best; small, fussy promontories are to be avoided as they usually lack stability and dry out very quickly during spells of drought. If there is room, a broad, shallow 'S' shape is very effective.

Cemented brick or dressed stone-sided beds should have a foundation. This need not be elaborate. Dig out a trench 30cm (1ft) wide by 15cm (6in)

and fill with a cement ballast mix. Alternatively, the trench can be 30cm (1ft) deep and filled with rammed ballast. Where the soil is loose (very peaty or sandy), you should build a foundation of this sort for natural stone beds as well.

Brick and stone beds with cemented joints can be built with vertical sides, but make sure as the building proceeds that you leave gaps for plants. Growing plants on the sides is a major attraction of the raised bed. Shaped timber, such as railway sleepers, can be built up vertically, but the inside corners should be secured with brackets or angle irons to prevent displacement.

Natural stone and timber beds should be stepped back to provide stability. It is necessary to fill them with the growing mix as building proceeds so that the whole structure is firm when completed.

Soil mixes When it comes to preparing a suitable growing medium, much depends on the range of plants you wish to grow. A good general purpose mixture can be made with two parts garden soil, one part peat and one part grit or very coarse sand. If the soil is of a clay nature, one part is enough. A handful of Growmore or bonemeal added to each barrow load will get the plants off to a good start. If lime-loving plants are to be grown, use limestone grit; if lime haters, then make sure your basic soil is not limy, and use an extra one to two parts peat. If the basic garden soil is not suitable use three or four parts peat and one of grit or sand plus the bonemeal.

The top of the raised bed can be set with nicely shaped pieces of natural stone and/or a 2-5cm (1in) layer of grit or fine gravel. Planting can now commence.

THE LOW PROFILE BED

A good compromise between the raised bed and the rock garden is the low profile or flat outcrop bed. This is best laid out informally and you can begin in the same way as for a natural stone raised bed. Natural stone is best, though irregular lumps of weathered cement or concrete can be used. Sandstone or limestone is recommended; smaller pieces can be used than those recommended for a rock garden as stability is not an important factor.

Once the outline is marked out, loosen the soil surface and fit together pieces of stone as closely as possible. Now fill the area within with chunks of stone – ideally fairly close together so that the completed bed is rather like three-dimensional crazy paving. The surface need not be totally level. For example, the largest pieces of stone can be used in the middle or at one end, thus giving the bed more character. The gaps and crevices can now be filled with a raised bed type mixture, firming it with a trowel or broom handle as work proceeds. Planting can be done as filling proceeds and this is the best way with narrow crevices. Topping the rooting mixture with coarse grit or gravel adds a pleasing touch and cuts down an early crop of weed seedlings. Such a rock bed provides

an excellent home for some of the more difficult bun and cushion-forming alpines, but serves equally well for a general collection of easy and colourful alpines.

A low profile or flat outcrop bed above, | constructed in limy sandstone.

1. Chunks of stone are fitted together to form a firm edge to the bed.

2. Once the outline rocks are in place, the centre is filled in with similar or larger pieces.

3. As soon as the rocks are in place, the gaps and crevices are filled with soil.

DRY WALLS

Anyone who has visited the upland regions to the west and north of the British Isles cannot fail to remark on the 'stone hedges' or drystone walls. They are very much a feature of the landscape and a splendid example of utilizing readily available local material. Although of purely utilitarian value, they are not without a certain aesthetic appeal. Much of this is the patina of lichens and mosses, and in favoured locations, the little ferns and other plants that colonize them.

Most dry walls are made of flattish pieces of stone, fitted together in jigsaw fashion with great skill, often with a protective capping of larger stones. In some areas, such as Cornwall, the walls are double thick with a core of soil. A thick covering of plant life soon forms on such walls.

The charm and utility of dry walls can be brought into the garden. Their use as dividers between one part of the garden and another, and their charm as a medium for growing rock and alpine plants, can make an intriguing garden feature.

A free-standing cavity dry wall packed with soil is, in essence, a linear raised bed and much of what has been said about building materials and construction also applies here. Brick and stone can both be used, though cemented brick is far from the spirit of an upland 'stone hedge'. It does, however, serve well enough and fits more successfully into the modern, formally designed garden. Whether brick or stone, cemented or not, small gaps should be left to provide homes for plants. As a wall needs to be even more stable than a raised bed, it is worth the extra trouble of providing a foundation for the first layer of stone or brick. There is much to be said also for planting up the smaller gaps as you build. Afterwards it can be a tricky job unless you prepare a batch of seedlings and rooted cuttings.

Retaining walls The drop below the edge of a terrace or raised patio provides an excellent way of gaining a dry wall and support for the soil behind. Generally the top will need to be capped by stone or turf, but the soil behind will never dry out and provides a good root hold for some of the larger choice rock plants.

A retaining wall (above) provides perfect drainage and shelter. Make sure the wall has a good foundation and leans slightly into the bank (left).

A steep slope makes a good site for a dry wall (right). Peg line at right angles to slope, dig along and below it.

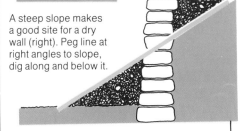

ALPINE LAWN

The home of the alpine lawn is above the tree line in mountains with a regular summer rainfall. The use of the word 'lawn' is a bit confusing – grasses are seldom dominant and the really smooth areas are often rather minimal between rock outcrops. The lawn effect is apparent in the closely woven, fairly even, dwarf-like nature of the vegetation. In actual fact it is an intricate mosaic comprising a wide range of small plants, diverse in both leaf shape and flower.

Regrettably it is not possible to duplicate an alpine lawn in lowland gardens. Quite a number of the plant components grow the way they do in response to climate and light intensity. In the garden they either grow larger and out of character or do not thrive at all. Nevertheless, there are quite a number of plants – not all true alpines – that stay low growing and co-habit happily together. From these, a very presentable and satisfying imitation of an alpine lawn can be created. Certain essentials must however be observed: the site must be sunny, the soil sharply drained and not over fertile. In fact, a fairly poor sandy soil gives the best results.

An alpine lawn of any size requires plenty of plants. Therefore, even a small lawn can be costly if all the plants have to be purchased. It is as well to think ahead and root many cuttings of the basic plants, bearing in mind that they will need setting out at 20-30cm (8-12in) apart each way. When planting, mix up all the chosen plants and set them out just as they come to hand. Here and there, plant small groups of one species to give character to the sward.

The biggest problem with an alpine lawn is weeds, and it pays to prepare the land well ahead by frequent hoeing throughout the summer or using herbicides at regu-

lar intervals. Perennial weeds must be eliminated at the outset or they will be a constant problem.

Ground level beds Using rock and alpine plants like miniature herbaceous perennials, to plant up ground-level beds, was introduced by Alan Bloom at Bressingham. The concept was to create trouble-free low level beds or broad edgings to larger borders. In many respects the overall effect is like the alpine lawn, but more formalized, with each plant species represented by a group of individuals. The plants are much more varied, some being larger than usual for an alpine lawn.

This way of using small plants can be varied in a number of ways. For example, larger groups or drifts of a few species can be used to create a dramatic effect. Small shrubs can be added as specimen plants to add height and interest. If some, or all of these, are evergreen, like dwarf conifers, then winter interest will be increased. Groups or drifts of the smaller bulbs look particularly effective coming through the low carpet of rock plants. An added attraction is a small pool which will allow the culture of miniature water lilies and other small water plants.

LEFT A corner of a small alpine lawn with a mosaic of raoulias, globularia, drabas and stonecrops.
ABOVE A wide range of rock and alpine plants grown in a flat site.
RIGHT Plant mosaic in a ground level bed. Associating well are: *Sedum ochroleucum*, *Veronica* selleri, *Sempervivum* 'Rubin', a *Phlox subulata* hybrid and *Dianthus pungens* (the last two in the foreground are not in bloom).

THE PAVED GARDEN

Garnishing a paved patio, barbeque area or terrace with rock plants to add a little life to the sterile expanse of stone is a regular practice and is to be commended. Creating a paved area entirely for the culture of rock and alpine plants is not widely undertaken, and yet it is easily done and very worthwhile.

As with the rock garden, scree and alpine lawn, a paved garden has its equivalent in the wild. Furthermore, you do not need to go abroad to see excellent examples. The geological feature known as limestone pavement is well developed in northern England (for example, at Ingleborough) and western Ireland (The Burren). Limestone pavement is aptly named; it is smooth, hard, grey to grey-white rock, criss-crossed with crevices of varying depths known as grikes. If not over-grazed, such areas support a wide variety of not only low-growing perennials, but shrubs and trees as well. They are in fact one of the most satisfying of wild areas for the gardener.

Limestone is not essential in the garden; any stone slabs can be used. Even broken street paving, obtainable from some local councils, is an acceptable substitute. A flat or slightly sloping, well-drained site is necessary though. Perennial weeds must be eliminated and the surface raked level. If the soil is on the heavy (clayish) side it is best to spread 5cm (2in) of coarse sand or grit on the surface and fork or cultivate it into the top 10cm (4in) or so. After raking, more sand can be spread over the surface and left. The paving is now laid direct, butting some pieces closely together, but leaving plenty of good gaps for plants. Avoid creating cracks too

LEFT Part of a totally paved garden in May, with *Euphorbia myrsinites* as a centrepiece. A wide range of alpine and bulbous plants are grown in crevices.
ABOVE Natural limestone pavement at Scar Close, Ingleborough; note the smooth surface and plant-filled grikes.
RIGHT A wider view of the paved garden on the left, but soon after it was completed. Shrubs, annuals and perennials take their place with the rock plants.

small to plant, as these will soon sprout annual weed seedlings.

Once the slabs are laid, planting can begin. Although the temptation is great, avoid using too many plants. If at the end the slabs are completely obscured much of the character of this facet of gardening is lost. Unlike the alpine lawn and ground-level beds, each plant in paving should be viewed as an individual and needs its background of stone. Mat, hummock and cushion-forming plants look especially good in paving and a wide range of different sorts can be grown. Indeed, if we follow the limestone pavement example, at least some small shrubs and larger perennials should be chosen. Dwarf bulbs look good and thrive if planted in the larger gaps. In particular, choose autumn and winter flowering species to provide colour during the 'dead' months. Species *crocus*, *iris*, *scilla* and *tulipa* are particularly worthwhile. As the foliage fades, or ideally just before, sow some of the small choice annuals to close the gaps. Cream-cups (*Platystemon californicum*), violet cress (*Ionopsidium acaule*), baby blue eyes (*Nemophila menziesii* (syn.*insignis*)) and sun plant (*Portulaca grandiflora*) are all excellent for this purpose. Avoid the highly-bred bedding annuals which look out of place when mixed with rock and alpine plants and miniature shrubs.

CONTAINERS

Not unnaturally, miniature plants demand miniature gardens. The Chinese have long made tiny gardens in ceramic and stone containers, but it was only early this century that the idea really caught on in the British Isles. Firstly, natural stone sinks, troughs and querns were used, but as these became scarce, modern glazed sinks were modified and mock stone ones made. Recently, pottery containers in a variety of shapes and sizes have come to the fore.

Creating a sink garden can give a great deal of satisfaction, allowing plenty of scope for artistic and cultural skills. How one sets about it is a very personal thing, but the best gardens invariably result when soil, rocks and plants are blended to imitate part of a mountain ledge or outcrop. Each container can be designed to suit a particular group of plants, for example steeply creviced outcrops for the tiny androsaces and other rock-face plants, or gravel or very low profile rocks for the mat-formers.

There are several modifications of the basic sink gardening ideas. The slab garden uses flat pieces of stone, generally square to rectangular, with small, irregular stones cemented around the edges to hold the soil. The centre is then landscaped as for a sink. Slab gardens are usually raised up on pillars.

Tufa lump gardens are made in single blocks of this fascinating and attractive stone. Each lump should not be less than a football in volume, preferably larger. Tufa is formed when calcium bicarbonate solution, leached by rain from existing limestone rocks, flows across a hillside or arises as a petrifying spring. Where this solution flows through loose, well-aerated, decayed vegetation, the calcite precipitates to fill all the interstices. Later, the vegetable remains disappear, leaving a network of channels and crevices. Tufa varies much in its hardness and can be whitish or tinted reddish or yellowish with iron oxides. It provides a unique rooting medium much

Provided the soil is sharply drained, shallow sinks and containers do not need special drainage material. However, sinks deeper than 23-30cm (9-12in), are best if a layer of fine rubble or coarse gravel is placed in the bottom. Whatever the depth of the container, it must have several small, or one or two large, drainage holes.

appreciated by many alpines. Despite its calcite composition it is surprising how well some calcifuge plants thrive on and in it. Many otherwise difficult plants can be grown successfully on a tufa lump. Although it is a soft stone, it is fairly resistant to weathering and soon forms a tough 'skin' on broken surfaces. Planting holes are easily made with a manual or powered drill. On vertical faces the holes should angle downwards to aid percolation of water. Seedlings and rooted cuttings of very small plants must be used and carefully packed into the holes with a gritty mixture. The tufa gardens should be displayed on trays of moist coarse sand.

Tufa is expensive and not too easy to come by, but a substitute known as hypertufa is easily made. The ingredients are two parts dry moss peat, passed through a 6mm (¼in) sieve, one part coarse sand and one part cement. After thorough mixing, add water until a stiff dough-like consistency is obtained. Irregular lumps should be shaped and allowed to firm for a week. Planting holes can be made with blunt sticks just before the material hardens.

Hypertufa can also be used to make a mock stone sink. A wooden box of the right size is thickly coated inside with the mixture, then a smaller box is pushed down onto it to keep it in place during the hardening process. Glazed sinks can also be transformed with a coating of hypertufa. First the sink is coated with a bonding agent, or the glaze is roughened with a powered masonry drill. The hypertufa mixture is then patted on about 12mm (½in) thick, leaving a rough, stone-like surface. It is surprising how quickly the surface of hypertufa weathers and looks natural.

ABOVE A modern glazed sink covered with hypertufa to create the appearance of soft limestone or tufa. Among the stonecrops and houseleeks are the yellow-flowered *Draba bryoides* and the pale blue *Anemone obtusiloba*.
RIGHT A sink or trough made of hypertufa with a centre-piece of *Dianthus* 'La Bourbrille'.

THE ALPINE HOUSE

The idea of growing alpine plants under glass often strikes the novice as curious. Why grow plants of the high mountains in the protected environment of a greenhouse? Most true alpines are buried under snow all winter and need a completely dormant cold rest period. The alternating cold and mild spells of a temperate lowland winter, together with rain rather than snow, upsets their biology. Sometimes they fail to flower, or do so in a very inferior way; some fail to thrive or grow at all.

The more equable climate of a greenhouse, where alpine plants can be kept dry overhead, seems to compensate for lack of snow cover and flowers develop normally, though often ahead of the usual time.

Rock plants from coastal areas or more southerly climates are not always hardy and fare better with the winter protection a greenhouse affords. Some, though hardy enough, also have woolly foliage which is less likely to spoil or rot with a glass cover overhead. This brings us to the major advantage and attraction of the alpine house – the enjoyment of winter and early spring flowers and young foliage that is unsullied by mud splash and frost. Furthermore,

LEFT Pans of *Tecophilaea cyanocrocus* and cultivars plunged in sand-filled benches. ABOVE Lumps of tufa, grouped to form an outcrop on an alpine house bench, with plants set between and into the faces of the stone. Tufa is the perfect medium for many of the more difficult alpines.

the plants are much closer to eye level – even more so than on a raised bed.

There are also cultural considerations: most rock and alpine plants respond well to pot culture and the enthusiast can formulate different composts – humus rich, gritty, loamy, acid, alkaline – to suit individual requirements. As a glance

along the competition benches of an Alpine Garden Society Show clearly demonstrates, some of the finest specimens are grown in pots and pans.

Type of greenhouse There are two essentials when choosing a greenhouse to be used as an alpine-house, the best possible ventilation and good light. Ideally, there should be continuous ventilators along the ridge, preferably on both sides. There should also be a series of vents at ground and bench level. When choosing a site the greatest amount of winter light possible should be aimed for. Certainly a location away from the shade of trees and buildings is essential unless plants needing shade are of primary interest. Strong benching must be installed to support the weight of a substantial layer of fine gravel and all the pots and pans of compost. Iron, concrete or brick piers make the strongest supports, with stout aluminium or galvanised iron sheeting to hold the gravel and plants. Ideally, bench tops with 15cm (6in) deep edging should be constructed and filled with gravel. Pots and pans can then be plunged as far up to their rims as possible, keeping the roots cool and setting off the plants to perfection.

In much of Britain, where the weather is mild, it is not necessary to provide the plants with heat. However, a heater of some sort should be available in case of an exceptionally cold spell or hard winter. The heater is used merely to prevent the temperature dropping too far below freezing point. It must be recognised that even in the mountains, plants beneath deep snow seldom get their roots hard frozen. The root systems of many plants are much less hardy than their tops. If there is to be a succession of plants in bloom or good foliage throughout the year, a frame, more or less equal in square area to the greenhouse, will be a most useful adjunct. The plants that are resting, or not in bloom, can be plunged into this. In summer the tops are completely removed so that the plants can mature and ripen in unobstructed sunlight and natural rainfall. If you cannot afford a frame, then a sand, gravel or weathered-ash plunge bed should be constructed where spare plants and those not in bloom can be kept.

Providing the soil is well-drained, and light is adequate, a wide range of rock and alpine plants can be grown with the minimum of attention. The only real and essential chore is to keep smothering weeds at bay. As with all other plant groups however, attention to certain basic cultural details will ensure that growth is vigorous and healthy and flowers profuse.

Drainage True rock and alpine plants will not stand stagnant water around their roots, hence the need for impeccable drainage. If the natural soil is sticky clay, work in plenty of coarse sand, grit or fine gravel. Ideally, construct scree, shingle or raised beds or make rock outcrops above the natural soil surface.

Containers, particularly troughs and sinks, must have good-sized drainage holes in the bottom. These are covered with a layer of crocks to prevent the soil from washing through. Some growers use a lot of drainage material, including gravel and soil sievings, but if the rooting medium is properly made this is not necessary.

There are many composts for container plants. The comments made about scree mixtures are relevant here (see pages 14/15). A good all-purpose mix is one part loam, one part peat and one part grit or coarse sand. Even equal parts peat and grit are satisfactory providing regular feeding is carried out.

Feeding the rock garden If the basic soil is a good fertile loam, feeding can be minimal, but it should not be ignored. A dressing of good general fertilizer such as Growmore should be applied each alternate year – or annually on the poorer soils. Alternatively, one of the slow-release general fertilisers can be used at half the recommended application.

Scree and raised beds Plants grown in the very free-draining, scree-type mixtures soon starve once they reach maturity, so a regular feeding is essential. Remember that in the wild, scree plants are continually being supplied with rock dust, washed down by rain and melted snow. This dust contains

A raised bed makes an attractive feature for the garden and is an ideal way of growing alpine plants as it is easy to provide the good drainage needed. This one has been planted with a mixture of dwarf conifers (see page 45) and hummock-forming plants (see pages 42-3).

1. Only plant alpines when the soil is nicely moist. start by digging a hole wider than the root ball.

2. Set the plant in the middle of the hole and carefully fill in around. Firm with the fingers.

3. Smooth the soil around and top off with a 1.5-2cm (½-¾in) layer of grit or fine gravel.

essential minerals and is in effect a natural fertiliser.

Containers Feeding is even more essential for the small volumes of soil contained in a pot, sink or other container and these should be attended to regularly. Some of the more leafy, vigorous rock plants in pots will benefit from a dose of ICI Liquid Growmore at half strength every three to four weeks during the growing season.

Top dressing All the cultural situations in which one can accommodate alpine and rock plants will benefit from a light top dressing now and then. Top dressings can be either fresh soil, made-up compost or sieved leaf mould, or peat plus a little fertiliser. They are usually applied in early spring. First, a thin layer of old soil is removed from around the plants, then the top dressing is spread to bring the level to what it was before. About 12mm (½in) is all that is required around alpines. Using a sterile (pasteurised) potting compost or pure moss peat will ensure that weeding for the ensuing season is down to a minimum.

The alpine house A totally different cultural regime is needed for the alpine house. Attention must also be paid to the ventilation, shading and watering. During the summer, the plants need full ventilation at all times, unless gales are imminent. The aim must be to keep conditions as cool as possible. In sunny areas, or in prolonged spells of sunny weather, it may be necessary to screen the hottest rays by lightly shading the glass with a colour wash or blinds. Strips of nylon net curtain can also be used to good effect. Do not rely too heavily on shading however, for cushion and hummock plants and others of congested growth soon grow out of character. Alpines will stand heat providing there is plenty of air movement around them. It is better to invest in an extractor fan, or to leave a fan heater running with the heat off, than to shade unnecessarily.

Watering must be carried out freely during warm weather, but more carefully during dull, cool periods. In winter, keep the compost just moist unless, as with some early bulbous plants, there is active growth.

PROPAGATION

Plenty of satisfaction can be had from propagating your own plants, either to increase a particular favourite or to give away to friends. Happily, a wide range of rock and alpine plants can be multiplied with the minimum of care and equipment.

Propagation can be carried out in a variety of ways, but seeds, cuttings and division are the most useful and widely used. Cuttings are especially important and for them some sort of propagating case or frame is necessary. Most useful of all is a small cold frame with a 7.5-10cm (3-4 in) layer of coarse sand in the bottom. This is known as a sand frame and there are few alpines which cannot be rooted in it. Alternatively a sand bed can be made in a partially shaded site and each batch of cuttings covered with a closed cloche, or hoops of strong galvanised wire (old coat-hangers can be used) supporting polythene sheeting. Opaque white sheeting is best – clear sheeting or glass will need light shading until rooting commences.

Cuttings These are either whole shoots – stems plus leaves – or pieces, trimmed and inserted with one-third of their length in the rooting medium. Many rock and alpine plants are raised from basal cuttings. These are the shoots that arise at ground level or just above. In some cases they arise on the bases of flowering stems. These shoots are carefully pulled off with a backwards and downwards motion or cut with a razor blade or sharp knife. The lowest leaves are removed and the cutting inserted. Basal cuttings are also known as heel cuttings as each one has a base or 'heel' of tissue from the parent stem. Larger plants, such as rock rose (*helianthemum*) and penstemon are propagated from stem tips. These are cut just beneath a leaf or leaf pair and are known as nodal cuttings.

Whichever type of cutting is used, remove all but six leaves, (fewer if they are relatively large and broad, like arabis, more if they are very small, such as thymes). If there are too many leaves, they will not get enough moisture and may wilt; too few leaves will cut down the photosynthesing area and delay rooting. It is wise to use a hormone rooting powder, such as 'Keriroot', just prior to insertion. This will ensure rooting, and the included fungicide will stop early decay. Late summer is the best time to take cuttings, but many basal shoots are ready in spring. When well rooted – shown by new growth at the tips – the cuttings can be planted in situ or potted singly until the following spring.

Division All the well-known rock and alpine plants of tufted or clump-forming growth are suited to this method. A mature plant is dug up and carefully pulled apart with the fingers, making sure that each piece has healthy roots and shoots. Sometimes a knife point is needed to sever a tough stem or root. Very dense clumps may have to be divided by the levering action of two hand-forks thrust into the middle, back-to-back. Divisions must be planted or potted immediately. Spring or early autumn is the best time.

Seed This is the basic means by which all true flowering plants in-

1. Stem tip cuttings should be severed at the point where the tissues start to become firm.

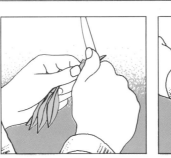

2. After removing the lower foliage, insert in a cuttings compost up to the lowest leaf.

3. Cushion saxifrages and similar plants can be broken up into small divisions.

4. The divisions should be treated as large Irishman's cuttings, placing several in a pan or box until well rooted.

5. The seed of rock and alpine plants is best sown in small pots, half pots or pans.

6. After firming the compost with the bottom of another pot, sow the seed thinly and cover with a thin layer of grit.

crease and spread. Seeds are encapsulated embryo plants with a limited food store. They are geared to germinate when the season is right for seedling growth – usually spring, but sometimes later.

The seeds of alpines mainly ripen in autumn when it would be unwise for tiny seedlings to emerge. Evolution has provided most of them with a dormancy period which is broken by a period of cold (winter), so germination occurs naturally in spring and not before. For this reason it is recommended to sow alpines as soon as ripe, or in autumn and winter, and to leave them outside to experience at least six to eight weeks chilly weather; actual freezing is not always needed. Alternatively, put the sown seed in the refrigerator for this short period, then bring into warmth. Rock and alpine seed is best sown in small pots – 5-7.5cm (2-3in) is usually large enough. The pots are filled to within 1cm (¾in) from the top with a standard seed sowing compost, ideally mixed with one third extra sand or perlite. Sow the seed thinly on the surface and cover with a 5mm (⅕in) layer of fine grit. Place outside in a peat or sand bed and water regularly during dry spells. Lowland rock plants can be kept in a frame or greenhouse and then sown in spring.

PESTS AND DISEASES

All plants are prone to attacks by insects and other animals and fungal parasites. Happily, alpine and rock plants are not particularly susceptible and many are never afflicted. The main pest and disease symptoms and their causes are listed on the facing page.

If the attack warrants spraying with an insecticide or fungicide, bear in mind that before opening the container it is important to read the instructions carefully and then follow them to the letter. Use the recommended dose rate and do not use extra for 'luck', as too strong a concentration may damage the plants while a weaker solution is unlikely to kill the pest or disease. Ideally spray in the morning or evening, avoiding the hottest part of the day, at least during the summer.

Rust disease attacking Sempervivum. Affected leaves become longer and thinner, and the rosettes develop a more erect appearance.

SYMPTOMS AND TREATMENTS

Leaves Deformed Slightly or severely deformed leaves are usually the result of damage by aphids (green and blackfly). These are tiny, soft-bodied oval insects that often occur in dense colonies. There are also yellow, pinkish and greyish sorts, some of which are winged. If the leaves are also tattered and/or have irregular holes, then capsid bugs are the culprits. They are like larger, flatter aphids, but they are faster and more stealthy. Spray both pests with 'Sybol' or 'Picket'.

Leaves eaten Leaves with pieces eaten out of them usually mean that caterpillars, earwigs, slugs or snails have been feeding. A regular notching of the leaves of dwarf evergreen shrubs indicates vine and clay-coloured weevils at work. 'Sybol' can be used against all but slugs and snails – these need a bait based upon metaldehyde or methiocarb. Caterpillars can also be killed by 'Sybol' or 'Picket'. Removing by hand is also worthwhile if damage is slight.

Leaves mottled and yellowing Plants in the alpine house, and those grown close to warm, sheltered walls, may suffer from attacks by red spider mite. These pests suck the sap and cause a lightish mottling followed by yellowing and/or browning, then premature falling. This must be combated as early as possible by spraying with 'Sybol'. Dwarf conifers in more open sites may show symptoms similar to those of red spider mite, but more severe. This is caused by the conifer spinning mite and can be treated with repeat applications of 'Sybol'.

Leaves with spittle-like masses In the late spring and early summer, the white frothy masses of the froghopper grub (nymph) sometimes occur on rock plants. This sucking insect weakens the plant and can cause stunting. Both the nymphs and the froth can be washed off with a jet of water from a hose. For complete eradication use a jet spray of 'Sybol'.

Leaves wholly or partly removed or shredded Woolly or grey, hairy-leaved plants are frequently taken by starlings, sparrows and other birds for nest building. Achilleas, artemisias and *Chrysanthemum* (*Tanacetum*) *haradjanii* are particular favourites. The only sure way of saving the plants is to cover them with cotton thread or netting. Make sure the thread is cotton, as nylon does not break easily and can trap a bird by the legs.

Seedlings collapsing Densely sown seedlings can collapse at ground level and die. This is caused by damping off disease, which in turn is aggravated by overcrowding and over-moist conditions. No one fungicide is totally effective, but spraying with Benlate + 'Activex' at 7-10 day intervals prevents further trouble. Watering must be done with more care and, in the future, sow seed more thinly.

Whole plant wilting and failing to thrive Pot-grown plants, particularly those in the alpine house, may be infected with root aphids. These are covered with a white waxy powder, easily seen when the plant is knocked out of its pot. Watering with spray-strength 'Sybol' is the most effective measure. Later, the soil should be washed from the roots and the plant repotted.

The list of plants that follows is arranged according to their use. All are commercially available, though some may have to be searched for.

BEGINNERS' ROCK GARDEN PLANTS

ALYSSUM
Madwort
A large genus containing several garden-worthy plants, mainly with yellow flowers and hoary to grey leaves. Best known is *A.saxatile* (gold dust) from central and south-east Europe. It forms wide hummocks 20cm (8in) tall and opens its bright yellow flowers in spring. *A.s.*'Citrinum' is lemon-yellow, 'Dudley Neville' is biscuit-yellow. Other species are *A.montanum* (white), and *A.wulfenianum*.

CAMPANULA
Bellflower
This varied and decorative genus contains plants with bell and star-shaped flowers in shades of blue, purple and white. *C.carpatica* from the Carpathian Mountains, forms clumps up to 20cm (8in) tall with blue bells in summer; *C.c.*'Alba' and 'Bressingham White' are white; 'Blue Clips' has extra large blooms; 'Blue Moonlight' is palest blue. Other easy species: *C.poscharskyana*; *C.cochlearifolia* (*pusilla*).

Campanula portenschlagiana

GERANIUM
Cranesbill
Not to be confused with pot geranium (*Pelargonium*), the hardy cranesbill genus contains several good rock plants in shades of pink, red, purple, blue and white. *G.cinereum* 'Ballerina' was raised at Bressingham. It grows 15cm (6in) tall and spreads more widely with white flowers heavily feathered crimson-purple from late spring to autumn. Other easy cranesbills include *G.himalayense* (*grandiflorum*) 'Alpinum', *G.×* 'Russell Prichard' and *G.sanguineum lancastriense*.

DIANTHUS
Pink
Many of the familiar garden pinks are easy and showy, others are choice and more difficult. *Dianthus deltoides* (maiden pink) from Europe thrives practically everywhere. Above mats of dark green leaves it produces 15-25cm (6-10in) stems of deep pink flowers in summer. *D.d.*'Albus' is white, 'Signal Light' is glowing crimson, and 'Wisley' has bronzy leaves and deep crimson blooms. Other easy pinks: *D.gratianopolitanus* (*caesius*), *D.× arvernensis*, *D.plumarius* and hybrids.

SAXIFRAGA
Rockfoil
This large, mainly mountain genus is one of the rock gardener's 'musts'. *S.X apiculata* forms cushions to 30cm (1ft) wide, studded in spring with yellow flowers on 6cm (2½in) stems *S.× a.* 'Alba' is white. Other easy species are *S.moschata*, *S.paniculata* (*aizoon*).

Geranium dalmaticum (top)

Dianthus deltoides 'Signal Light'

VIOLA
Violet and pansy
Many of the small species and forms of violets and pansies make splendid rock garden subjects. *V.cornuta* from the Pyrenees is one of the easiest and longest living species. It forms hummocky mats and elegant, long-petalled violets in shades of mauve to purple-blue from late spring to autumn. *V.c.*'Alba' is white, 'Grovemount Blue' is sky-blue and *V.c.minor* is much smaller and more compact in growth. Other easy violas: *V.labradorica* 'Purpurea', *V.septentrionalis*.

Viola cornuta minor

PLANTS FOR SHADE

CYCLAMEN
Sowbread
All the hardy cyclamen species are splendid for shady spots in the rock garden and elsewhere. *C.coum* (E.Mediterranean) is valuable for its late winter flowers which vary from pale to rich purple-pink. These are carried on 5-7.5cm (2-3in) stems above dark green leaves, The forms sometimes listed as *C.atkinsii*, *orbiculatum* and *vernum* have silvery-patterned foliage. Other species include *C.europaeum* (*purpurascens*) and *C.neapolitanum* (*hederifolium*).

Cyclamen coum

GENTIANA
Gentian
Many members of this large genus are mountain plants and rank among the jewels of the alpine regions. No rock garden should be without one. *G.sino-ornata* (from Western China and Tibet) is prostrate with bright blue, yellow-green striped flowers in autumn. It needs lime-free moist soil and partial shade.

HABERLEA
This mountain relative of the tropical gesneriads (e.g. saintpaulia and streptocarpus) favours north facing banks and crevices. It makes tufts of evergreen primrose-like leaves and produces foxglove-like blooms in spring. *H.rhodopensis* (Greece, Bulgaria) has lilac flowers on 10-13cm (4-5in) stems. *H.r.ferdinandi-coburgii* is larger in all its parts; *H.r.virginalis* is white.

PRIMULA
Primrose
Few large genera have so much to offer the general gardener and alpine specialist. Certainly no rock garden, scree or raised bed should be without them. *P.sieboldii* (Japan) is a woodlander with attractive long-stalked leaves and heads of primrose-like flowers of pink and purple in spring. *P.s.*'Alba' is white. Other shade primroses include *P.denticulata, P.× pruhoniciana (P.× juliana)* 'Tawny Port', 'Wanda', *P.vialii, P.vulgaris.*

SHORTIA
This small genus of choice plants is perfect for a shady bed of leaf mould or peat. Those cultivated have attractive evergreen leaves and pink or white bell-shaped blooms in spring and early summer. *S.soldanelloides* (Japan) forms small mats of dark foliage and produces clusters of pink, deeply fringed bells on 7.5cm (3in) stems. Other easy species: *S.galacifolia* and *S.uniflora.*

Primula sieboldii 'Alba'

VIOLA
Violet
Most of the true violets are excellent shade plants. *V.septentrionalis* (north-east North America) is a clump-forming species, growing to 13cm (5in) tall. It blooms profusely in spring and is usually violet-purple, but lilac and white forms are grown. Other species include *V.papilionacea, V.cucculata.*

SCREE, SHINGLE-BED, PAVING

ANDROSACE
Rock jasmine
Most of the species in this genus are true alpines, some of them very choice and difficult to grow. They are members of the primrose family and their small, but profusely borne flowers show the resemblance. *A.sarmentosa (A.primuloides sarmentosa)* forms mats of large, pale green rosettes in summer, woolly button-like rosettes in winter. The pink flowers on 7.5-10cm (3-4in) stems open in spring. Other species: *A.lanuginosa* and *A.sempervivoides.*

COTULA
Pincushion
Most of these mat-forming plants are apt to be invasive, though their mossy carpets are decorative. *C.atrata* (New Zealand) is perhaps the choicest and neatest, with the largest flower heads in deep crimson and white. *C.a.luteola* is the usual cultivated form with cream and pink heads on 5cm (2in) stems in spring and summer. Other species: *C.potentillina, C.squalida.*

LEONTOPODIUM
Edelweiss
The 20 kinds of edelweiss are all very similar. They are intriguing

rather than beautiful. Tiny groundsel-like flower heads are surrounded by white to yellowish, woolly bracts imitating petals. *L.alpinum* (Europe) forms tufted mats of narrow leaves and 15-25cm (6-10in) stems that bear white bracts in summer. *L.a.*'Mignon' is more compact. Other species: *L.palibinianum.*

PENSTEMON
Beard tongue
This large American genus is typified by freely-borne, foxglove-like flowers in a wide range of colours. The dwarf sorts are first-rate scree plants, but they are apt to be short lived. *P.pinifolius* (south-west USA, Mexico) is very distinct in its needle-like leaves. It forms mats of wiry stems and carries scarlet flowers on 15-20cm (6-8in) stems in summer. Other species: *P.roezlii, P.rupicola, P.scouleri.*

PHLOX
There are few duds among the 60 species in this genus and the mat-formers are indispensable rock gardener plants. *P.douglasii* (*P.austromontana*) from West USA forms mats up to 45cm (1½ft) wide which are smothered with lavender, pink or white flowers in spring. Several cultivars are obtainable, mainly of hybrid origin which include red and crimson blooms. Other species: *P.borealis, P.×* 'Chattahoochee', *P.×* 'Millstream', *P.subulata.*

RAOULIA
Excellent mat and cushion plants; no scree is complete without at least one member of this largely New Zealand genus. *R.australis* is one of the easiest, forming dense flat mats of tiny silvery leaves in summer studded by stemless yellow groundsel heads. Other species: *R.glabra, R.hookeri, R.tenuicaulis.*

Androsace sarmentosa

Raoulia australis

DRY WALLS, VERTICAL CREVICES

CAMPANULA
Bellflower
There are bellflowers for all sites in the garden where rock plants are grown. *C.portenschlagiana* (*muralis*) (Yugoslavia) is a first-rate species for the dry wall, but it needs room to travel. From summer to autumn it produces lilac-blue flowers in abundance. Other bellflowers are *C.garganica*, *C.poscharskyana* and *C.×* 'Birch Hybrid'.

ERINUS ALPINUS
Fairy foxglove
This is the only member of its genus and it is not unlike the tiniest foxglove, about 10cm (4in) tall. A native of the Alps and Pyrenees, it is an evergreen perennial, producing its rose-purple flowers in spring and summer. *E.a.albus* is pure white; 'Dr Hanaele' is carmine and 'Mrs Boyle', soft pink.

GERANIUM
Cranesbill
Several of the small cranesbills look lovely in a dry wall and none better than *G.dalmaticum* (Yugoslavia). This choice species forms hummocks to 30cm (1ft) wide, freely set with quite large, rich clear pink flowers in summer. *G.d.*'Album' is white.

Geranium 'Ballerina'

HELIANTHEMUM
Rock rose
The mat-forming members of this genus are fine for banks and walls, but they also thrive on the flat. *H.nummularium* (Europe) and its hybrids grow to 40-60cm (16-24in) or more when hanging from a wall. In early summer they are covered with double or single flowers like tiny roses. *H.n.*'Amy Baring' is orange-gold and compact, 'Fire Dragon' is orange-red; 'Butterball' is double yellow; 'The Bride' pure white and 'Wisley Primrose', single yellow.

HYPERICUM
St Johns wort
This huge world-wide genus contains some gems for the rock garden, all yellow flowered. Perfect for a wall is *H.olympicum* (Balkan Peninsula) with its 30-45cm (1-1½ft) wide hummocks of small grey-green leaves and profuse bright yellow blossom in summer. Other species: *H.cerastoides* (*rhodoppeum*), *H.polyphyllum* and *H.trichocaulon*.

Hypericum olympicum

Arenaria montana (right)

Sempervivum atachnoideum (below)

ALPINE LAWNS AND GROUND-LEVEL BEDS

SAXIFRAGA
Rockfoil
Many rockfoils are crevice plants in the wild, none more so than *S.callosa (lingulata) lantoscana*. It forms cushions of narrow silvery encrusted leaves from which appear 30-45cm (1-1½ft) long, down-arching plumes of white flowers in spring. Other species for walls: *S.cotyledon*, *S.longifolia*.

SEMPERVIVUM
Houseleek
This genus of hardy succulent plants is made for walls and crevices, and all the known species and hybrids are suitable. *S.arachnoideum* is the prettiest – each small reddish-green rosette is neatly webbed with white hairs. In summer, 7.5-13cm (3-5in) tall stems bear starry rose-red flowers. Other species: *S.ciliosum*, *S.grandiflorum*, *S.montanum*, *S.pittonii*, *S.tectorum* and varieties.

ACAENA
New Zealand Burr
Several members of this southern hemisphere genus are vigorous mat-formers and can be used as key plants in an alpine lawn. *A.microphylla* (New Zealand) has tiny, somewhat ferny, often bronze-tinted leaves and almost stemless, bright red burrs in summer. Other species: *A.buchananii*, *A.caesiiglauca (glauca)*, *A.novae-zealandiae*, *A.*'Purple Carpet'.

ARENARIA
Sandwort
Both weeds and choice rock plants are contained in this large genus of small species. *A.montana* (Western Europe) is one of the largest flowered, carrying its pure white blossom over loose mats of narrow, greyish-green leaves in spring and summer. Other species: *A.balearica*, *A.purpurascens*.

GENTIANA
Gentian
Various trumpet gentians stud the alpine turf in spring, but in the garden, only the stronger species can hold their own among alpine meadow plants. *G.acaulis* (*excisa, kochiana*) from Europe is one of the best, eventually forming clumps to 20cm (8in) or more wide. In spring, rich blue flowers open, sometimes in profusion, sometimes rather sparsely, but they are always brilliantly attractive. Other species: *G.angustifolia, G.clusii.*

HERNIARIA
Rupturewort
The mat-forming plants in this genus are modest and have no floral charms. They are, however, a cheerful green and make good alpine lawn fillers. *H.glabra* (Europe, Asia) is the best species, with tiny bright green, glossy leaves. Other species: *H.ciliolata.*

THYMUS
These tiny, wiry-stemmed sub-shrubs and shrubs are indispensable in the alpine lawn. *T.praecox arcticus* (Europe) is usually listed under its alternative names, *T.drucei* and *T.serpyllum.* It is a mat-former, growing to 45cm (1½ft) or so wide with tiny, smooth or hairy leaves and a profusion of tiny

Gentiana acaulis (kochiana)

tubular flowers in summer.
T.p.a.'Albus' is pure white, 'Annie Hall' is flesh-pink, 'Coccineus' has dark foliage and crimson flowers, 'Lanuginosus' has hairy grey leaves and pink flowers, 'Pink Chintz' is salmon pink.

VERONICA
Speedwell
The mat-forming speedwells are valuable alpine lawn plants, providing pleasing foliage and quantities of pure blue flowers. *V.cinerea* (Turkey) has narrow grey leaves and pale blue flowers in summer. Other species: *V.austriaca, V.pectinata, V.prostrata.*

Thymus serpyllum

TROUGHS AND SINKS

DIANTHUS
Pink
Several of the small mountain pinks are perfect for sinks and other small containers. *D.neglectus* (*pavonius*) (south-western Europe) forms small cushions of green to grey-green leaves above which are carried buff buds and pink to crimson flowers on 10cm (4in) stems in summer. Other species: *D.alpinus, D.callizonus, D.haematocalyx.*

GENTIAN VERNA
Spring gentian
This widespread European gentian is the best for sinks and smaller

containers, being rarely more than 5cm (2in) tall. Unlike the familiar trumpet kinds, it has small starry flowers but they are even more brilliant deep blue. *G.v.angulosa* is larger in all its parts with a winged, somewhat inflated, calyx.

POLYGALA
Milkwort
This huge, largely tropical genus yields several attractive mountain plants. *P.chamaebuxus* (central Europe) is a small evergreen shrublet rarely more than 15cm (6in) wide and 10cm (4in) tall. Carried off and on throughout the year, the yellow flowers are pea-like, but with two prominent wing petals. *P.c.*'Grandiflora' ('Purpurea') has purple wing petals.

PRIMULA
Primrose
Several small members of this genus are rock crevice plants and both thrive and look well in containers. *P.marginata* (south-western Alps) has pretty, white-edged, round-toothed leaves and clusters of blue-lilac, primrose flowers in spring. Other species: *P.auricula*, *P.hirsuta* (*rubra*), *P.× pubescens*.

SAXIFRAGA
Rockfoil
Most of the smaller hummock-forming saxifrages make good sink plants, being attractive in foliage and flower. *S.sancta* (Greece) is sometimes listed under *S.juniperifolia*. It forms tight hummocks of bright green leaves set with head-like clusters of small yellow flowers on 2-4cm (¾-1½in) tall stems in spring. Other species: *S.burserana*, *S.× irvingii*, *S.marginata*.

SEDUM
Stonecrop
This huge genus of succulent plants of the northern hemisphere contains many run-of-the-mill rock plants and a few gems for containers. *S.hidakanum* (Japan) forms loose clumps of small bluish leaves and rose-red flower clusters in late summer and autumn. Other species: *S.cauticolum*, *S.spathulifolium*.

Polygala chamaebuxus 'Grandiflorus'

Saxifraga juniperifolia 'Sancta'

DWARF BULBS

CROCUS
No collection of bulbs for the rock garden would be complete without some spring and autumn flowering crocus. *C.aureus*, (Yugoslavia to Turkey), though commonly planted, is still one of the best orange-yellow to yellow species for the late winter. *C.speciosus* (Turkey) is the finest of the early autumn sorts, its 10-12cm (4-4½in) tall lilac to purple-blue flowers opening before the leaves. Other species: *C.zonatus* (*kotschyanus*), *C.goulimyi* (autumn), *C.imperati*, *C.chrysanthus*, *C.sieberi* (winter spring).

IRIS
This large genus contains a few tiny 7.5-10cm (3-4in) tall winter-spring blooming species indispensable for the rock garden. *I.histrioides major* (Turkey) is the best, with large purple-blue blooms opening before the leaves in late winter. Other species: *I.danfordiae*, *I.reticulata*.

NARCISSUS
Mini narcissi and daffodils are always appealing and look especially well on the rock garden. *N.triandrus albus* (Portugal, western Spain) is best known as 'angel's tears'. It grows to 13cm (5in) tall and opens nodding white flowers in spring. *N.t.concolor* is yellow. Other species: *N.bulbocodium*, *N.asturiensis* (*minimus*). *N.cyclamineus*, *N.rupicola*.

SCILLA
Squill
This genus provides shades of blue, a colour not common in the early part of the year. *S.sibirica* (Turkey, Iran, Caucasus) has glossy strap-shaped leaves and 10-15cm (4-6in) tall spikes of wide, bright blue bells in early spring. Other species: *S.bifolia*, *S.tubergeniana*.

TULIPA
Tulip
Several tulip species are small enough for the rock garden and have great charm. *T.tarda* (Turkestan) has rosettes of narrow glossy green leaves and clusters of bright yellow, white-tipped flowers in early spring. It rarely exceeds 10cm (4in) in height. Other species: *T.clusiana*, *T.linifolia*, *T.pulchella*, *T.kaufmanniana*, *T.batalinii*.

Crocus aureus

Tulipa tarda

DWARF SHRUBS

ABIES BALSAMEA HUDSONIA (North America)

This neat, rounded, slightly flat-topped dwarf conifer is one of the best of its type for the rock garden. It has rich, bright green leaves when happily situated, but needs a moist, acid to neutral soil to look its best. It grows about 2.5cm (1in) annually.

Abies balsamea 'Hudsonia'

CRYPTOMERIA JAPONICA VILMORINIANA (Japan)

The Japanese cedar has given rise to several dwarf mutants, but none is more useful on the rock garden than this one. It forms a dense globe of rigid shoots set with tiny leaves which turn purplish in winter. It grows about 15mm (½in) per year. Other cultivars: 'Bandi-sugi', 'Jindai-sugi', 'Pygmaea'.

HEBE OCHRACEA

(New Zealand)

This is one of the shrubby veronicas classified as 'whipcord' with leaves reduced to scales and resembling a conifers. It forms a characteristic spreading bush, flat-topped when young, but rounding with age. It takes at least 10 years to reach 60cm (2ft). The whole bush appears to be lacquered in old gold. Small white flowers, often in profusion, are borne in summer.

Salix boydii

JUNIPERUS COMMUNIS COMPRESSA (North temperate zone).

Undoubtedly the best known dwarf conifer, this juniper forms dense columns of prickle-tipped, grey-green leaves rarely above 60cm (2ft) tall. It grows about 12mm (½in) per year, sometimes more in favoured areas. It needs a sheltered site and can be browned in hard winters.

PHYLLODOCE CAERULEA

(circumpolar)

A member of the heather family, this diminutive bush grows 15cm (6in) tall by 20-30cm (8-12in) wide. It has dark green, yew-like foliage and terminal clusters of nodding, purple, urn-shaped flowers in summer.

SALIX × BOYDII (Scotland)

Probably a hybrid between the Lapland (*S.lapponum*) and net-leaved (*S.reticulata*) willows, *S.× boydii* forms a curiously attractive gnarled shrublet, growing eventually to 60cm (2ft) or more. It has rounded, corrugated leaves that are grey and downy when young. It grows 12-25mm (½-1in) a year, but somewhat faster when young.

ALPINE HOUSE

ANDROSACE CYLINDRICA
(Pyrenees)
Although this charming species can be grown in the scree it responds to alpine house treatment, especially if planted in a lump of tufa. It forms smooth, small grey-green hummocks which are spangled with almost stemless white (rarely pink) flowers in spring.

CALCEOLARIA
Slipper-wort
This large South American genus with its curiously attractive pouched flowers, yields several desirable species for the rock garden and alpine house. $C. \times$ 'John Innes' (*C.biflora × polyrrhiza*) is a vigorous plant ideal for a large pan, producing large yellow flowers in abundance on 15cm (6in) stems in early summer. Other species: *C.darwinii, C.biflora, C.polyrrhiza.*

LEWISIA
Bitter-root
All 16 members of this genus are native to Western North America. They form rosettes of narrow, fleshy leaves and bear clusters of often showy, somewhat daisy-like flowers. *L.tweedyi* is evergreen and in spring and summer produces branching sheaves of salmon-pink flowers, each one 5cm (2in) wide. Other species: *L.columbiana, L.cotyledon, L.howellii, L.rediviva.*

PRIMULA ALLIONII
(Maritime and Ligurian Alps)
This primula grows in vertical crevices at low altitudes in dry areas, and therefore needs an alpine house to thrive. It forms low cushions of sticky-downy leaves that make a pleasing foil for the shortly stalked, pink to red-purple flowers in spring. *P.a.*'Avalanche' is pure white. This is not a difficult species to grow provided the foliage is kept dry and repotting is carried out annually or biennially, just after flowering.

RHODOHYPOXIS (S. Africa)
This is a small genus of bulbous plants which can be grown as perennials, flowering as they do from late spring to early autumn. Re-potting should be carried out every two to three years. *R.baurii* produces tufts of 5cm (2in) long narrow hairy leaves and clusters of starry flowers in shades of red, pink and white. Named cultivars and mixed seedlings are available.

SAXIFRAGA BURSERIANA
(E.Alps)
This species flowers in late winter and early spring when the weather can be wet and cold. In an alpine house its pure white flowers can be enjoyed in perfect condition. It is hummock-forming with tiny silvered leaves which are attractive all the year. *S.b.*'Gloria' and 'Major' have larger flowers and there are several hybrids with smaller yellow or pink blooms.

Calceolaria 'John Innes'

46

NOT SO EASY ROCK GARDEN PLANTS

CYPRIPEDIUM
Slipper orchid
The 50 members of this genus are mainly hardy, but need partial or dappled shade and a compost composed largely of leaf mould or peat. *C.reginae* is known as Showy Lady's Slipper in its native eastern North America. It grows 30cm (1ft) or more in height, with pleated pale green leaves and solitary or paired white and rose flowers in early summer. Other species: *C.acaule*, *C.calceolus*.

CYANANTHUS
This genus is a member of the bellflower family. The species cultivated are prostrate with up-turned tubular flowers having five spreading petals. Neutral to acid soil rich in peat or leaf mould is necessary. *C.microphyllus* (Himalaya) spreads 30-45cm (1-1½ft) from a central rootstock. Violet-blue flowers open in autumn. Other species: *C.lobatus*.

DRABA
Whitlow grass
Most of the garden worthy members of this genus form attractive hummocks of tiny leaves, above which hover tiny four-petalled yellow and white flowers in late winter or spring. *D.bryoides* (*D.rigida*) makes firm cushions rarely more than 7.5cm (3in) wide. Bright yellow flowers appear on thread-like 5cm (2in) tall stems in spring and sometimes later. Other species: *D.dedeana* (white), *D.polytricha*, *D.longisiliqua*.

EDRAIANTHUS
This genus could be mistaken for a bellflower and is a member of the same family. *E.pumilio* (Yugoslavia) is the choicest and smallest, forming small hummocks of short, grassy, grey-green leaves upon which sit upward-facing purple blue bells in summer. Other species: *E.dalmaticus*, *E.gramifolius*, *E.serpyllifolius*.

HELICHRYSUM
Everlasting
This very large and varied genus includes a few choice species, best grown under glass. *H.milfordiae* (*H.marginatum*) forms very decorative mats or low cushions made of tiny silvery-haired rosettes. White, sometimes crimson-tipped, everlasting flowers appear on short stems in summer. Other species: *H.coralloides*, *H.selago*.

PRIMULA PETIOLARIS
(Himalaya)
This desirable primrose is the type plant of a group known as Petiolaris primulas. All like a moist, but well-drained soil, rich in humus, and a partially shaded site. *P.petiolaris* has tufts of deep green pointed-toothed leaves and deep pink flowers with a white eye, in winter and spring. Other Petiolaris species: *P.gracilipes*, *P.edgeworthii*, *P.whitei*.

Primula petiolaris

INDEX AND ACKNOWLEDGEMENTS

Picture credits

All pictures courtesy of Gillian Beckett

Artwork by

Richard Prideaux & Steve Sandilands